THE BABYLONIAN CONCEPTION
OF HEAVEN AND HELL

BY

DR. ALFRED JEREMIAS

THE
BABYLONIAN CONCEPTION OF HEAVEN AND HELL

BY

ALFRED JEREMIAS, Ph.D.

PASTOR OF THE LUTHERAN CHURCH

AUTHOR OF "BABYLONISCH-ASSYRISCHEN VORSTELLUNGEN
VOM LEBEN NACH DEM TODE,"
AND OF THE ARTICLES
"IZDUBAR," "ISHTAR," ETC., IN ROSCHER'S "LEXICON"

TRANSLATED BY J. HUTCHISON

WIPF & STOCK · Eugene, Oregon

Wipf and Stock Publishers
199 W 8th Ave, Suite 3
Eugene, OR 97401

The Babylonian Conception of Heaven and Hell
By Jeremias, Alfred
ISBN 13: 978-1-60608-421-2
Publication date 12/30/2008
Previously published by David Nutt, 1902

CONTENTS

	PAGE
I. INTRODUCTION	1
II. DEATH AND BURIAL	4
1. Man's Inevitable Fate	5
2. Mourning Customs	11
3. Funerary Rites	12
4. Refusal of Funerary Rites	14
5. Places of Burial	16
III. THE WORLD OF THE DEAD	18
1. Place of the Underworld	19
2. The River of Death	19
3. Representations of Hades	20
4. Deities of the Underworld	23
5. Demons of the Underworld	25
6. The Underworld and Vegetation	27
IV. NECROMANCY	28
V. SALVATION FROM "THE LAND WITHOUT RETURN"	31

CONTENTS

	PAGE
VI. JOURNEY OF GILGAMESH TO "THE ISLAND OF THE BLESSED"	34
VII. THE PARADISE OF THE FIRST OF MANKIND IN ERIDU	39
VIII. FOOD AND WATER OF LIFE IN THE BABYLONIAN PARADISE	42
IX. CONCLUSION: PSYCHOLOGY OF THE BABYLONIAN CONCEPTIONS OF HADES .	47

THE BABYLONIAN CONCEPTION OF HEAVEN AND HELL

Introduction.

No consecutive account of the Babylonian religion can as yet be given, nor will it for many years come within the range of possibilities to achieve it. Abundant fragments of Babylonian religious and mythological literature have indeed been brought to light by the excavations of the last few years, and by dint of strenuous efforts a large proportion has been classified and deciphered. But extending as they do over a period of more than three thousand years it is in comparatively few cases that these fragments can be set in chronological order. The preservation of most of the religious texts known to us is due to the collecting zeal of the Assyrian king Asurbanipal (668–626 B.C.) at whose command copies of the literary monuments of Babylonia were made on clay tablets by the royal scribes. Magnificent

INTRODUCTION

material for the investigation of Babylonian thought will be available if, in a happy future, the interrupted excavations in the library of Nineveh should ever be completed, but as yet only a small portion of the contents has been recovered and in a greatly damaged condition. Even then our knowledge of the Babylonian religion would still be lacking in essential data, namely the traditionary lore of the temples: this it is which would throw light on the histories of the different cults.

In the following pages we have attempted to set forth the Babylonian conceptions of a future life, but it must be borne in mind that fragmentary material only is available for the purpose. When once the temple of Nergal at Kutha shall have been excavated much more will certainly be known regarding Babylonian eschatology than is the case at present. Nevertheless it is precisely this particular department of the religion that lends itself most easily to any attempt at systematic representation by us. The sacerdotal religion of Babylonia took little heed of the next world, presenting in this respect a marked contrast to Egyptian thought. The gods of Babylonian worship were, on the whole, gods of practical life, even Nergal of Kutha being in the first place a lord of the living. It was thus left to the imagination of the people to brood over thoughts of life after death, and apparently the mythological fragments that have been preserved restore these somewhat persistent popular conceptions in their main outlines.

The reader will be struck by the surprising correspondence between the Babylonian ideas concerning death and Hades and Jewish notions of the same. The connection of Israel with Babylonia was indeed of the closest, and the Tell el Amarna tablets have proved that Babylonian thought had spread over the land of Canaan before it was conquered by the Hebrews. At the time these were written there stood in Jerusalem a temple of the Babylonian Storm-god, Ninib. In more than one traditional version of the Hebrew stories of patriarchs Babylonia is cited as the original home of the people of the Bible, and during both Monarchy and Exile Babylonian culture played among the Israelites a part similar to that played by French culture in Germany in the eighteenth century. It would seem as though the gloomy conception of life in the underworld was the common heritage of Babylonians and Israelites from primitive Semitic times.*

* A detailed handling of the existing material with philological treatment of the cuneiform documents may be found in the author's "Babylonisch-Assyrischen Vorstellungen vom Leben nach dem Tode" (Hinrichs, Leipzig), of which a new and fully revised edition is in preparation.

Death and Burial.

To the Babylonian death was the "inevitable," "night-like" fate, which "in accordance with primæval law" brings to an end all human glory. All his prayers were for long life, old age, and terrestrial immortality in his posterity. "Make my years to endure like the bricks of Ibarra, prolong them into eternity," prayed Nebuchadnezzar. An ancient blessing ran:

" Anu and Anatu in heaven bless him ;
  Bel and Beltis in Ekur grant unto him the lot of (long) life ;
  Ea and Damkina in ocean give unto him life of long years ! "

It is told in the legendary story of one of the heroes of ancient Babylonia how he found a plant the eating of which restored the aged to youth. "Dear life" might be lengthened out by conduct well-pleasing to the gods. Tiglath Pilesar says of his grandfather : " The work of his hands and his sacrifices were well pleasing to the gods, and thus he attained unto extreme old age." Nabonidos, the last Chaldæan-Babylonian king, prays to the Moongod: "Keep me from sin against thy great Godhead, and a life of far-off days grant unto me as a gift," while for Belsazar, his first born, he prays : " Cause the fear of thy sublime godhead to dwell in his heart that he consent not to sin ; may he be

MAN'S INEVITABLE FATE

satisfied with abundance of life!" The formal curses at the end of the royal inscriptions show, on the other hand, that destruction of posterity and sudden death were regarded as punishments for offences against gods and men. He who should destroy the inscriptions of Tiglath Pilesar is threatened as follows: "May the god Ramman command that he live not a day longer. Let his name and seed be exterminated out of the land." "So long as heaven and earth endure be his seed destroyed," runs another terrible curse: "his name blotted out, his posterity overthrown, may his life end in hunger and misery, may his corpse be cast out, no burial shall it receive."

None, however, could ultimately escape the fate of death. Sudden and unexpected dawns the day "that sets not free." "Life is cut off like a reed." "He who at evening is living, in the morning he is dead." Many a man dies on a day that was not "the day of his fate." The lot, the fate of man being determined by the gods in the chamber of destiny, hence the day of death was known as the "day of fate"; of one who died it was said "the day of his fate tore him away," but of a suicide: "Terror overpowered him, and he went to death by his own will, not by that of the gods." No herb grown might be the antidote of death; no spell could avail against it. "So long as we build houses," says the

Babylonian Noah, "so long as we seal (*i.e.*, conclude treaties), so long as brothers quarrel, so long as there is hatred on earth, so long as rivers swell in flood, . . . no image (for purposes of exorcism?) will be made of death."

The laments over the lot and doom of death are often striking. In one of the religious texts from the library of Asurbanipal we read of one "the joy of whose heart is the fear of the gods," and to whom, nevertheless, "the day is sighing, the night weeping, the month wailing, the year lamentation: . . . Into dark bonds was I cast; a dagger pierced me; the wound was deep; . . . in the night it suffered me not to breathe freely for a moment; my joints were torn and loosened; on my couch . . . as a bull, as a sheep, was I wet with my urine; . . . no exorciser expelled my sickness; no priest put an end to my infirmity; no god helped; none took my hand; no god had compassion on me; no goddess came to my side; the grave was open; . . . ere I was yet dead was the funeral dirge due." . . . Then at length redemption drew nigh. Another instance runs as follows: "Death is the covering of my couch; already have I struck up the lament (lit., tones of the flute)." It is in keeping with the character of Babylonian mourning that at a certain episode in the story of the Flood, Istar "shrieked like a woman in travail, because the corpses of

ISTAR'S JOURNEY IN HADES

mankind filled the sea like fish spawn." "The gods wept with her over the Anunaki, the gods lay crouched (at the celestial lattice of Anu); they abode there weeping, their lips firmly closed."

Again and again the Babylonian legends give poetic utterance to the thought that all splendour vanishes, all strength fails before the might of death. "The Journey of Istar in Hades" tells how life died away on earth when the goddess sank into the Underworld. Even the death goddess mourns and "sinks down like a reed that is cut through," and says:

". . . instead of bread, earth will I eat, instead of
  wine . . . will I drink,
 for the men will I weep, who leave their wives,
 for the women will I weep, who [turn] from the
  loins of their husbands,
 for the little children will I weep, who before their
  time [make an end?]
 Go, watchman, open to her the gate,
 Seize her, according to the laws of old."

For by these laws all adornment must be left behind, and naked must man pass into the world of the dead.

The first gate he let her pass; he divested her, taking the great crown from off her head.

"Wherefore, O! warder, takest thou the great crown from off my head?"

"Enter, lady, for such is the decree of the death goddess."

The second gate he let her pass; he divested her, taking from her ears the jewels.

"Wherefore, O! warder, takest thou from my ears the jewels?"

"Enter, lady, for such is the decree of the death goddess."

The third gate he let her pass; he divested her, taking from off her neck the chain.

"Wherefore, O! warder, takest thou from off my neck the chain?"

"Enter, lady, for such is the decree of the death goddess."

The fourth gate he let her pass; he divested her, taking away the ornaments from her bosom.

"Wherefore, O! warder, takest thou away from my bosom the ornaments?"

"Enter, lady, for such is the decree of the death goddess."

The fifth gate he let her pass; he divested her, taking the jewelled girdle from her loins.

"Wherefore, O! warder, takest thou from my loins the jewelled girdle?"

"Enter, lady, for such is the decree of the death goddess."

The sixth gate he let her pass; he divested her, taking the bangles from her wrists and ankles.

LAMENT OF GILGAMESH

"Wherefore, O! warder, takest thou from my wrists and ankles the bangles?"

"Enter, lady, for such is the decree of the death goddess."

The seventh gate he let her pass; he divested her, taking from her body the garment.

"Wherefore, O! warder, takest thou from my body the garment?"

"Enter, lady, for such is the decree of the death goddess."

When it is told further how she was smitten with sickness in the eyes, sickness in the loins, sickness in the feet, sickness in the heart, sickness in the head, this is doubtless meant to indicate that death is the destruction of all the senses, and that all that is of the body must fall to corruption.

A passage in the Gilgamesh epic, extremely interesting for the history of civilisation and usually* interpreted as a lament by Gilgamesh over his friend Eabani, runs: "To a temple [no more thou goest] in white garments [no more thou clothest thyself] . . . with perfumed fat of bulls no more thou anointest thyself, so that men crowd round thee for the fragrance; the bow thou no longer settest on the ground (to draw it),

* In his recent translation, however, Jensen takes a different view.

those who were wounded by the bow surround thee; the sceptre no more thou carriest in thine hand, the spirits of the dead ban (?) thee; bangles no more thou puttest upon thine ankles, no (war-) cry raisest thou evermore on earth; thy wife whom thou lovedst thou kissest no more; thy wife whom thou hatedst thou smitest no more; thy daughter whom thou lovedst thou kissest no more; thy daughter whom thou hatedst thou smitest no more, the woe of the Underworld hath seized upon thee."

The misery of death was a special theme of song at the rites of mourning for the spring god Tammuz (Adonis), who each year sank into the world of the dead at the approach of winter. One lament for Tammuz recalls to mind the gardens and flower-pots used in the Phœnician and Greek Adonis cult, the forced growth and rapid fading of the plants. It runs: "Thou shepherd and lord, spouse of Istar, king of the Underworld, king of the dwelling-place of the waters; thou O shepherd art a seed corn that drank no water in the furrow, whose germ bore no fruit in the field, a young sapling that has not been planted by the water course, a sapling, whose root has been cut, a plant that drank no water in the furrow." In another Tammuz dirge we read: "Thou treadest (?) the closed way, the path without return . . . he departed, descended to

FUNERARY RITES

the bosom of the Underworld . . . the Sun-god sent him down to the land of the dead, with lamentations was he filled on the day when he fell into great tribulation, in the month that let not his life come to completion, on the path where all is at end for man ('that brings the children of men to rest,' adds the scribe), to the wailing of the deed, he, the hero, to the far off invisible land."

Some little knowledge of Babylonian funeral customs can be gained from the scenes and inscriptions. The corpse was preserved by means of milk, honey, oil, and salt; it was swathed in linen, strewn with spices, and laid on a stone bier. In the so-called Hades reliefs the forearms of the corpse point upward. Wailers, both male and female, are in attendance at the funeral, lamenting and playing the flute; the relatives are present in "rent garments" or in mourning garb; libations, incense, dirges, prayers, and perhaps animal sacrifices forming part of the rites. On the reverse side of an unpublished fragment from the library of Asurbanipal, the obverse of which represents a royal burial, is the inscription: "The wives lamented, the friends replied," pointing evidently to the use on such occasions of antiphonal singing between men and women.

The accompanying action and gestures were

violent as with all Orientals. The mourner wept, rent his garments, tore or shaved off his hair, cast himself down upon the ground (see Job i. 20), scarred his face, beat his loins. In the annals of Sargon it is said of a mourning Babylonian: "He fell down upon the ground, rent his garment, took the razor, broke forth into wailing."

Babylonians and Assyrians buried their dead; with them as with the Hebrews the burning of the corpse, except in case of necessity, was reckoned indignity and disgrace. The "vulture stela" found in the ruins of Ur of the Chaldees represents in one of its reliefs the burial of those slain in battle. Kings and great nobles were buried in temples and palaces, while the graves of the common people lay without the city. The ancient Babylonian king Gudea states incidentally that he has built the temple according to the Number Fifty, and erected within it a mausoleum of cedar wood. It would seem, therefore, that Babylonian temples like the Egyptian pyramids conceal beneath them royal tombs. Another majestic place of burial was the palace of Sargon I., a king famous in legend; certain of the Kassite kings were buried " in the palace of Sargon." In the annals of Asurbanipal mention is made of cemeteries at Babylon, Sippar, and Kutha, and Sanherib tells how a flood in the little river Tebilti had so disturbed the royal tombs in the midst of Nineveh as to lay bare the sarcophagi. Great care was lavished on furnishing the graves of the rich and the great. The Assyrian fragment mentioned above (page 11) describes the funeral ceremonies at the death of a king. "In royal oil I laid him, with meet solemnity, the gate of his grave, of his place of rest have I closed with strong copper and have made fast his . . . Vessels of gold and silver, all that pertains to the furnishing of the tomb, (also) the emblems of his authority which he loved have I presented before the Sun god and laid them in his grave with the father who begat me. Gifts gave I to the princes, to the Anunaki, and to the gods who inhabit the earth," *i.e.*, the Underworld. Drinking vessels and dishes of food for the dead were not only laid with them in the tomb, but were also placed upon it. Special care was taken to supply the manes of the dead with water to drink, and to this end apparently cisterns were made in the cemeteries. "If the dead have none to care for him," concludes the Twelve Tablet epic, "then is he consumed by gnawing hunger, vainly he languishes for refreshment; what is cast out on the street that he eats." The libations, regularly offered on the anniversary of death, formed the most important item in the worship of the dead, and the responsibility for offering them rested in the first place on the surviving son. In a deed fixing a boundary any man who should remove the boundary stone is cursed as follows: "May Ninib, lord of landmarks, rob him of his son, the Water-pourer." The commemoration day of the dead is called "the day of the feast of the dead," "day of dejection," "day of lamentatation," "day of mourning." The *nak me* priests, or "water pourers," performed the libation rites at the graves. "At the mourning festival of libations to the manes of my royal ancestors," says Asurbanipal, "I put on the garments of mourning and bestowed a boon on gods and men, on the dead and on the living." To this is added a penitential prayer spoken by the king at the graves of his ancestors. In his annals, however, he tells us that to his slain enemies he denied the Dirge of the Water-pourer. Bloody sacrifices of vengeance were also made at the tomb. The same king relates how he ordered prisoners of war to be slaughtered near to a colossal bull, on the scene of the murder of his grandfather Sanherib, as a solemn festival in honour of the deceased monarch.

To be deprived of the prescribed rites of burial was regarded as a terrible thing. The curse on him who should destroy the sacred inscriptions of the Assyrian kings is: "In famine shall his life end, his corpse shall be cast out and receive no

REFUSAL OF FUNERARY RITES

burial." Elsewhere we are told that burial rites were refused to a rebel who had committed suicide. When conquered foes were to be treated with special ignominy the tombs of their ancestors were destroyed that the repose of the dead within them might be disturbed, and the prophecy of Jeremiah (viii. 1, *cf.* Baruch ii. 24) that the bones of the Jewish kings, priests, prophets, and citizens will be taken from their graves and scattered beneath the sun is in strict accordance with the cruel war customs of Babylonians and Assyrians. Asurbanipal tells how after the overthrow of Elam he destroyed the sanctuaries of the land, and then uncovered and ravaged the mausoleums of the kings; "their bones I carried with me to Assyria, unrest laid I on their shades, and cut them off from the funerary rites of libation." King Sanherib was not satisfied with carrying off by ship the property and subjects of Merodachbaladan, he must needs also bring out from their mausoleum the bones of that unhappy king's predecessors. Again we are told how conquered kings, confined in the notorious Cage which stood to the east of Nineveh, were compelled for the special delectation of the populace to break in pieces the bones of their ancestors. No wonder many kings chose the sites of their tombs in the inaccessible swamps of the Euphrates, better to protect their sepulchres from profanation: so says Arrian, and his statement is supported by the inscriptions.

It cannot be averred absolutely that any of the graves hitherto discovered in Mesopotamia are of primitive origin. Certainly the cemeteries discovered at Nimrud, Kuyundshik, and Khorsabad, are not Assyrian; as for Babylonian cemeteries there is no fixing of their date. In some tombs, such for example as the sepulchral mound discovered by Taylor among the ruins of Ur, the seal cylinders found indicate high antiquity. The mounds, which mark the sites of ancient cemeteries, have been kept so dry by means of careful drainage through clay pipes that the vaulting of the tombs and the clay sarcophagi are preserved in perfect condition. The tombs of Ur are those for which there is most reason to assume an Early Babylonian date. These are of two kinds: one type consists of an oval cover of clay, something like an inverted dish, about seven feet long, five feet high and two and a half feet broad; the other is a brick vault, seven feet long, five feet high, and three feet broad. Among the skeletons traces have been found of linen swathings, and in the tombs vessels of clay and copper, some of them containing the remains of date kernels. The massive cemented urns which were found containing remains of skeletons among the ruins of Warka

CEMETERIES

(Erekh) are undoubtedly of later date, perhaps belonging even to the Parthian period.

In 1887 Robert Koldewey, now director of a German excavation in the ruins of Babylon, chanced, during a short expedition in Surghul and El-Hiba (seven hours south-east of Shatra in the triangle formed by the Euphrates, Tigris and Shat-el-Hai), to discover two cemeteries containing dwellings for the dead, and massive tombs for the remains of bodies that had been burned. Examination of the ashes showed that the jewels of the women, the weapons, tools and seals of the men, and the playthings of the children, had been burned along with their bodies. Traces of animal sacrifices and of incense were recognised, as well as remains of vessels and food for the dead; there were also clay idols, human and animal. The many fountains discovered among the ruins of the cemetery testify to the zeal with which the dead were supplied with water for drinking. But these cinerary cemeteries are not Ancient Babylonian, as Koldewey would have us believe: the ancient Babylonians did not burn their dead.

Important conclusions as to Babylonian practices and beliefs in relation to death may be expected from the excavations at Niffer (Nippur). Observations made in the mounds of Niffer and Abu-Habba (Sippar) have shown that these ancient cities were divided into three sections: the temple quarter, the city of the living and the city of the dead.

The World of the Dead.

The specific name for the world of the dead was Aralu; poetically it was known as Kurnugia, *i.e., irsitum la tarat,* "land without return," "land of the dead," "the far-off land." The popular fancy conceived this place of the dead after the likeness of the tomb. Names such as Kigal, "vast (underground) dwelling," Unugi, "dark dwelling," designate both tomb and Underworld alike. Thus the earliest answer to the question "Where dwell the souls of the dead?" would be, "underground," and this explains the hyperbolic statements of the royal inscriptions that the foundations of their buildings rested on the bosom of the Underworld. To this also may be traced the description of the scorpion sphinxes, of which it is said that their heads reached to the vault of heaven and their breasts to beneath Aralu. Hence, also, in "Istar's Journey in Hades" lament is made that "Istar has gone down into the earth (Underworld) and has not returned." The entrance to this subterranean land lay in the west. We shall refer later to an exorcism in which the ghost is expressly relegated

PLACE OF THE UNDERWORLD 19

to the west that the warder of the Underworld may there retain him. Not only was the west the region of sunset and therefore of darkness; to the Babylonian it denoted the desert also, and for him the desert, as the sea, was alike a place of horror. The desert being, indeed, the battle-field and playground of demons, it is consistent with this view that the goddess Belit-Seri, "the lady of the desert," is brought into connection with the Underworld. The expression "far place," which occurs twice on one of the so-called Hades reliefs and is also used in exorcisms ("Let the sickness of the head fly away like a bird to the far place and the sick man be committed to the gracious hands of his god"), may be understood as a euphemism for the desert in the west as well as for hell.

The account of the journey of Gilgamesh to the "Island of the Blessed" speaks of the threatening "floods of death" in the south-east, in the Erythraean Sea. Again, in a formula for exorcism, the heart of the magician is to be overcome by "waters of death." These waters of death must have some connection with the "river of death" repeatedly mentioned in descriptions of the Underworld, and which is occasionally designated by the name Khubur. When a priestly magician says that he "has held back the boat and cut off the quay and thus prevented the enchantment of the whole world," the allusion is undoubtedly to events in the land of ghosts. The passage recalls the threat of Istar to shatter the Underworld and lead forth the dead into the world above to flock with the living. We are also reminded of the representation of the goddess of Hades on two of the Hades reliefs where the monster sails along the river of death kneeling in a boat. Considering the inconsistency of all such popular fancies it is hardly remarkable that, according to the Gilgamesh epic, the "waters of death" are in the south-east, though generally the entrance to the Underworld was supposed to lie in the west. Perhaps it was supposed that there were two approaches, one by land in the desert, another by the waters of the river of death.

Seven walls, pierced by seven (or according to one legend fourteen) gates, surrounded the place of the dead, sometimes represented as open country, sometimes as a city, sometimes as a huge palace, but always described as full of countless terrors. The opening part of the " Journey of Istar in Hades " is well known :

" Of the land without return, the land [. . .],
  thought Istar, daughter of the moon-god.
  The moon-god's daughter thought . . .
  of the house of darkness, the seat of Irkalla (*i.e.*, Nergal),

of the house, whence those who enter return not,
of the path which leads forth, but not back again,
of the house, wherein he who enters is deprived of light,
of the place where dust is their food, and clay their nourishment,
where light they see not, in darkness dwell they,
where they are clad in garments of wings as birds,
dust lies thick on door and bolt."

Still worse were the prospects held out to any specially unwelcome visitors. The queen of the shades says to the messenger from the gods who has forced his way into the Underworld: "With a great curse I will curse thee; the food in the gutters of the city shall be thy meat, the water in the sewers of the city shall be thy drink; the shadows of the wall thy dwelling, a threshold of stone thy seat; . . . shall break down thy strength." In another epic fragment this identical curse is directed against a captivating *hierodulos* who by her cunning brought bane upon one of the heroes.

The picture of the Underworld at the beginning of "Istar's Journey in Hades" is found almost word for word in an epic narrative belonging to the cycle of Gilgamesh legends; here, however, the continuation is remarkable. "In the house of dust, that I have trodden. . . . [there dwell] wearers of crowns who ruled the land from of old, there set forth . . . of Anu and Ea roasted meat, set baked meats [   ] with cold, with water from leather bottles; in the house of dust that I tread [dwell] *Enu*-priests and *Lagaru*-priests, there [dwell] exorcists and magicians, there [dwell] the anointed priests of the great gods, there dwell [the heroes] Etana and Ner, there dwells Erishkigal, queen of the Underworld, [there dwells] Belit-Seri, the scribe (female) of the Underworld bends before her." Then follows the account, unfortunately fragmentary, of what happened when the goddess Erishkigal raised her head and became aware of the intruder. The story certainly connects itself with the Gilgamesh epic, on the last tablet of which the hero entreats the ghost of his friend as it rises: "Tell me, oh! my friend, tell me, oh! my friend, what the Underworld is like; tell me." The spirit of his friend answers: "I cannot (?) tell it thee my friend, I cannot tell it thee; if I should tell thee what it is like . . . sit down and weep . . ." In the following lines, which alas! are fragmentary, he after all seems disposed to give his friend the information: "That wherein the heart (on earth) has rejoiced, that below is turned to dust."

In the midst of "the land without return" is a palace, whence the gods of Hades exercise their rule. According to the Babylonian Hades legends

DEITIES OF THE UNDERWORLD

the real power centred in a goddess called Allatu (*i.e.*, the "Mighty One"), or Erishkigal (*i.e.*, the "Mistress of the Great Place"). She is represented in the Hades reliefs as a lion-headed monster (perhaps as being the wife of the lion-god Nergal), kneeling on a horse in a boat, or—without boat—standing upon a horse, snakes in her hands and lions sucking at her breasts. The concluding portion of the Twelve Tablet epic, above referred to, says of her: "She who is dark (?), she who is dark, mother of Ninazu; she who is dark, whose gleaming shoulders (?) are hidden by no garment, whose bosom like to a . . . not . . ." This sombre goddess watches over the primæval laws of the Underworld, receives from the mouth of the porter the names of fresh arrivals, and upon those on whom her wrath falls pronounces the great curse. With the help of the Anunaki she jealously guards the spring (?) of life which is hidden in a certain sanctuary of the Underworld, the water of which can ravish the dead from her power, as was indeed one day about to happen. "Bending before her" stands a divine female scribe of the Underworld, of whose duties unfortunately we know nothing more definite. Among the servants of Erishkigal are prominent the often-named "watchman," or Chief Porter, and Namtar, the god of pestilence. Side by side with Erishkigal reigns, as king of

Hades, Nergal, god of war and pestilence. He is known as "lord of the tombs," "lord of the great city," "king of the river (of death)"; and ancient Babylonian texts call him "lord of the great land," "lord of the land without return." The special seat of his cult, the Babylonian city Kutha, became so closely identified with conceptions of Hades that in poetry the Underworld is actually called "Kutha." His temple in Kutha was regarded as the likeness of Hades, just as other temples were supposed to be in the likeness of the heavenly abodes of the gods worshipped in them. Among the clay tablets of Tell el Amarna is a Babylonian poem vividly describing the marriage of Erishkigal and Nergal. In some of its features the story recalls the Greek legend of Persephone: "Once when the gods were about to prepare a feast they sent a messenger to their sister Erishkigal to say to her, 'We must certainly descend to thee; if thou wilt not ascend to us, send one to receive thy portion of the feast.' Then Erishkigal sent Namtar, her servant." From further fragments of the story we learn that Nergal himself set out for the Underworld with twice seven assistants, bearing such names as Lightning, Fever, Fervent Heat, &c. The servants of Nergal were placed at the fourteen gates of the Underworld, and imperiously he ordered the watchman to admit them. Then in

DEMONS OF THE UNDERWORLD

conclusion we read, "Within the house he seized Erishkigal by the hair, bent her down from the throne to the ground in order to cut off her head. 'Slay me not, my brother, I have somewhat to say to thee.' Hearing this Nergal stayed his hand. She wept and sobbed (?) 'Thou shalt be my husband, I will be thy wife, I will give thee dominion in the vast Underworld; I will give into thine hands the tablet of wisdom, thou shalt be lord, I will be queen.' When Nergal heard this he seized her, kissed her, wiped away her tears and said: 'What thou ever askedst of me long months ago until now. . . .'"

In the train of Nergal, who himself was dreaded as the the god of pestilence (in this character known as Urragal), appear all evil spirits and demons. These demons were regarded as the offspring of Hades and said to be born in the west on the mountain of sunset, that is, they were supposed to exercise their activities by night. When the sun comes forth from the mountains on the east—says a poetical magic formula—and all the gods assemble in presence of the Sun-god, then the rays of the sun drive away the spectres. Elsewhere we are told that they exerted their evil powers from the desert; the desert which lay in the west of Babylonia, being supposed, as already noted, to be in close connection with the Underworld. "They shall withdraw afar, they shall retire from the city and descend into the earth (the Underworld)," says the exorcist. These demons of Hades were imagined as blood-devouring, blood-sucking monsters, not sparing even the images of the gods. Like serpents they glided into houses. "They take away the wife from her husband, tear the child from his father's bosom, drive the master away from his household." "From land to land they go, driving the maidens from their chambers, the son they lead away from the house of his parents-in-law, they drive the child from his father's house, they snatch the doves from the dove-cot, the bird out of its nest, they drive the swallows from their nests. They smite the oxen, they smite the lambs; mighty spirits (?), evil demons, hunters are they." "In the pastures they attack the folds, they bring sickness into the stalls of the horses, they fill the mouth of the asses with dust, they bring trouble into the stable of the she-asses." Almost every part of the body was threatened by its own special demon. *Ashakku* brought fever to the brain, *Namtar* threatened life with pestilence, *Utukku* attacked the throat, *Alu* the chest, *Ekimmu* the loins, *Rabiszu* the skin. *Labartu* was the nightmare, *Labaszu* epilepsy, while *Lilu* and *Lilit*, spirits known also to Jewish superstition, brought infirmities of the night. The words of Rev.

GODS OF FERTILITY

xviii. 2 are in exact accordance with fact as regards the Babylonian dread of spirits: " Babylon the great is become a habitation of devils, and a hold of every unclean spirit, and a hold of every unclean and hateful bird." Specially dreaded, as we have seen, were the sepulchral *Utukku* and *Ekimmu*, the ghosts of the dead. " They penetrate into the houses, seize upon man and cast him down in the night." There were many means of exorcism of which the most effective was to draw a picture of the demon and solemnly burn it. Of death alone no image could be made for this purpose. In a religious text occurs the passage:

> " High hold I the torch, put in the fire the images
> of *Uttuku*, of *Shedu*, of *Rabiszu*, of *Ekimmu*,
> of *Labartu*, of *Labassu*, of *Akhkhazu*,
> of *Lilu*, of *Lilitu*, of the maidservant of *Lilu*,
> of every foe that seizes on mankind . . .
> your smoke rise up to heaven,
> may sparks conceal the sun,
> your spells be broken by the priest, the son of the god Ea."

For the student of comparative religion the fact is specially noteworthy that among the Babylonians also the gods of the Underworld were closely allied with those of fertility and agriculture. The growth and decay of vegetation was brought into connection with the Underworld.

This is shown in the worship of Tammuz and in the invocations to the field-god Enmeshara. One of these invocations says: "Lord of the Underworld, sublime in Aralu (a name for Hades), lord of the place and of the land without return, mountain of the Anunaki, . . . great lord; without Ningirsu (god of agriculture) there is no success in field or watercourse and no germ is fertile!" The giant Eabani also, who, in the Gilgamesh epic, descends to the Underworld, is a god of the tilled fields (in this respect recalling Pan), and the hero Ner, who figures in one of the representations of the Underworld among the dwellers in Hades, is certainly identical with the field-god bearing the same name.

Necromancy.

Among the magic arts of the Babylonian priests necromancy undoubtedly held a prominent place. A series of mythological texts shows that scenes such as that between Saul and the witch of Endor were familiar to Babylonian fancy also. Among the lists of the various orders of priests we find the offices of "Exorcist of the spirits of the dead," the priest "who raises the spirit of the dead," and the *Sha'ilu*, the "enquirer of the dead."

The literature so far known to us has no example of the "enquiring of the dead." On the other hand, the ceremony for the raising of spirits seems to be described in the concluding lines of "Istar's Journey in Hades," though the exact meaning remains indeed somewhat doubtful. It is there stated in conclusion that at the feast of Tammuz the dead shall arise and breathe the fragrance of sacrifice. It may be concluded from this that the feast of Tammuz was celebrated by solemn invocations of the dead.

At the close of the Gilgamesh epic there is an instance of how such invocation was actually practised. On returning from his ancestor, Gilgamesh with his companion held solemn lamentation over his friend Eabani, who "verily has sunk down to the shades." "Every twenty miles they intoned the dirge (?), every thirty miles they held a festival in honour of the dead." With his dirge he went from one temple to another complaining that no evil malady had consumed his friend, that he had not fallen in the field of battle among men, but that the world of the dead had snatched him away. At last he turned to the god of the Underworld himself, to the "hero and lord" Nergal. Ea said to him, "'Knock at the chamber of the tomb (?) [open the earth that the spirit of Eabani may come forth from the Underworld].' [When] the hero Nergal heard this he knocked at the chamber of the tomb (?), opened the Underworld, and straightway let the spirit of

Eabani go forth from out the earth like a breath of wind."*

Thus then the ghosts of the dead were raised, but to rid oneself of ghosts that had been raised or that had escaped may well have appeared a more difficult matter. "I will raise the dead that they eat and live; more than the living shall the dead be," says Istar. To the Babylonians this was a terrible threat, for by them the shades from the Underworld were regarded as among the most malignant of evil demons. In one exorcism a sick man complains that the wizard and the witch have delivered him into the hands of a wandering ghost, and again the suffering of a man grievously ill is accounted for by the statement "the wicked ghost has come forth" (*i.e.*, from the Underworld). A collection of prayers of the time of Asurbanipal includes the prayer of a man possessed by a ghost. Complaint is made that the ghost will not loose his hold of the sick man day or night, so that his hair stands on end and his limbs are as if paralysed. The Sun god is entreated to free him from this demon, whether it be the shade of one of the family or that of some murdered man that is oppressing his being.

---

* This exorcism and indeed the whole Babylonian conception of the Underworld recalls the eleventh book of the "Odyssey," where the spirits of the dead are called by night to the Cimmerian shore, and wing their flight up to earth.

BELIEF IN IMMORTALITY

The sufferer has already bestowed on his tormentor clothes and shoes and a girdle, as well as a water skin and food for his departing journey. Now let him go to the West, to the Underworld, and there may the god Nedu, the gate-keeper of Hades, retain him fast that he escape no more.

SALVATION FROM THE "LAND WITHOUT RETURN."

In the light of the foregoing statements it can hardly be doubted that the Babylonians believed in personal immortality. The body decays in the grave (*shalamtu* is the name given to the corpse, that is to say, "that which is done with"), but the soul lives in the gloom of Hades, and in that abode of horror leads an immaterial, shadow-like existence. Their thoughts, however, took a further flight and conceived of a brighter fate. Diogenes Laertius appears to have been correctly informed in ascribing to the Babylonian schools of philosophy (or rather schools of the priests) a belief not only in immortality, but also to a certain extent in a resurrection.* We have

---

* The attention of the English reader is drawn to the fact, that according to Jensen's recent translation of the Gilgamesh epic, the Babylonian priests distinctly taught the doctrine of a resurrection, giving instances of its occurrence in order to strengthen the belief in a future life. Though the English edition of this pamphlet appears later than the German, it does not deal with Jensen's general conclusions.

already seen that to the gods of heaven was attributed the power in certain cases to shatter the whole realm of the dead, and also that in isolated instances the spirit of a dead man might be brought forth. The narrator of the "Journey of Istar in Hades," indicates in the mystic concluding lines of the poem what his auditor must do "if deliverance is refused," and earlier in the epic we are told how the goddess Istar herself is set free after the porter has been forced to sprinkle her with the "water of life." In the "eternal palace," however, the inmost sanctuary of the Underworld, there is a spring (?) of the water of life, guarded, apparently, by the Anunaki, already known to us as demons of the sepulchral world. Only indeed by violence and with the help of a special word of power of the god Ea can this water be reached. It was owing to the feast of Tammuz, who was condemned "to weep year after year," and whose return from the Underworld was celebrated annually, that the idea of deliverance from Hades had become one of the most widely diffused notions in the popular mind. The fact also that a whole series of divinities are distinguished by the epithet "raiser of the dead," is connected with the same order of ideas. It is, indeed, the Sun and Spring gods especially that are said to love to wake the dead. The statement was, therefore, due in the first place to experience of the

"THE RAISER OF THE DEAD"

renewal of nature in spring, though sometimes it was applied in a manner that cannot be misunderstood to the hope of mankind. Of Samas, the Sun god, it is said, "to make the dead live, to free the captive lies in thy hand." The god Nebo is praised as he "who lengthens the days of life and raises the dead." But above all it is Marduk, god of the Early Sun and of the Spring Sun who is spoken of as "the compassionate one, whose joy is in raising the dead," or simply—as on the last of the creation tablets—as "the raiser of the dead." In a charm against demons and sickness he is hailed as follows: "Thou compassionate one among the gods, thou compassionate one, thou who lovest to raise the dead, Marduk, king of heaven and earth, king of Babylon, lord of Esagila, king of Ezida, lord of the mighty house of life, heaven and earth are thine, the space or heaven and earth is thine, exorcism of life is thine, the saliva of life is thine, the pure exorcism of the ocean is thine, black-haired mankind, living creatures, as many as dwell on the earth, all the quarters of heaven, all spirits in heaven and earth [turn?] their ears to thee; thou art *Shedu*, thou art *Lamasu* (the spirit of protection and blessing), thou makest alive, thou bringest to peace, thou art the compassionate one among the gods . . . to thee will I devote myself." Cyrus caused it to be said of himself, after he had taken Babylon, the city of Marduk, that the inhabitants with one accord hailed him joyfully and greeted him with beaming countenances as "the lord who in the strength of him who calls the dead to life (*i.e.*, Marduk), had blessed them all with care and protection." The same power of "raising the dead" is attributed to Gula, the wife of Marduk, who moreover is called "the lady, raiser of the dead," and once mention is made of "the ship of the goddess Gula, the raiser of the dead." Curiously enough among the many theophoric proper names embodying divine epithets attributing life-giving power to a deity, there appears the name "Nergaluballith," *i.e.*, Nergal (god of Hades) makes alive."

The Journey of Gilgamesh to the Island of the Blessed.

The Twelve Tablet epic has also come down to us in fragments only. We know, however, that the hero of the story had, along with his gigantic friend, incurred the wrath and vengeance of the mighty goddess Istar. Eabani had died an ignominious death and gone down to Hades. Gilgamesh was smitten by terrible sickness, but was resolved not to die like his friend. Seized by the fear of death he fell wailing to the ground, but suddenly he conceived the bold resolve to

THE ENCHANTED GARDEN 35

hasten with all speed to his great ancestor, who had once dwelt in Suripak, but who had attained " the longed-for life in the assembly of the gods." Of him will he seek healing, find out the secret of immortality and also prepare the way for the deliverance of his friend Eabani. For this ancestor, as Gilgamesh tells us later, has the power to interpret life and death. The skin-clad wanderer travels far through awful ravines, and after manifold dangers from which the moon-god protects him, at length he reaches Mount Mashu. The entrance to the mountain is guarded by scorpion men of giant stature, whose wild appearance inspires him with such fear and horror that he loses consciousness. One of the monsters tries to dissuade him from the terrible journey, telling him that he must travel twelve miles through impenetrable darkness. At length, in response to his importunity, he opens the mountain door, and, after four-and-twenty hours of wandering, Gilgamesh stepped out into an enchanted garden, in which especially one divine tree so delighted him that he rushed up to it: "Precious stones it bears as fruit—the branches were hung with them, lapis lazuli it bears, fruits it bears, choice (?) to look upon." A divine mermaid, dwelling in a palace by the shore, put fresh difficulties before him. With threats and entreaties he sought to move her to show him the way to his progenitor and to give him a boat in which to cross the water. The mermaid warned him that never had ferry been there and that the Sun god only could cross the sea, for the waters of death are as a bolt shot to, barring all entrance to the Island of the Blessed. At length she betrayed to him where he might find the man who had ferried his ancestor across. Him Gilgamesh succeeded in persuading to his will, and after a terrible journey, minutely prepared for in advance, they reached the Waters of Death, having covered a distance of forty-five days' travel in three days. After exhausting work at the oars had brought them across these waters also, they approached the shores of the Fields of the Blessed. From the boat Gilgamesh complained to his ancestor of his woe, related his heroic adventures, bewailed the death of his friend and told how he had toiled over lands and mountains and had traversed all the seas without being able to cheer his countenance by any happy sight. After a long conversation discussing the inevitable and invincible mortal fate of man, Gilgamesh comes to his point and asks his ancestor how he had attained to his own happy lot. Then this favourite of the gods—no other than the Babylonian Noah—tells Gilgamesh, as he listens from his boat, the story of the Flood, which, as is well known, coincides in parts almost verbally with the biblical narrative

THE MAGIC PLANT

of the Deluge, but concludes with the removal of the rescued couple to a distant land, at the mouth of the rivers, where they live as the gods. After this tale Sit-napishtim (*i.e.*, "Germ of Life") promises Gilgamesh "the life that he strives after." He cast him into a sleep, with the help of his wife prepared for him enchanted food and treated him by seven magic processes. Then he caused his ferryman to take him to the enchanted fountain, where his boils were washed pure as snow, the sea carried away his leprous skin, and his whole body once more appeared sound and healthy. Before he returned there was revealed to him yet another particular secret, namely, that a magic plant grew on the island, the twigs of which gave secret power to men: whoever ate of it regained the strength of his youth. Gilgamesh got possession of the magic plant and in his joy named it *shebu-issakhir-amelu*, *i.e.*, "even when old a man becomes young again." Then Gilgamesh went back (by another route?) accompanied by the ferryman. Every twenty miles they chanted a dirge, every thirty miles they held a feast in honour of the dead. Whilst Gilgamesh was drawing water (for purposes of libation?) from a spring the magic plant slipped from his grasp and a serpent known as the "earth lion" seized it from him. In his terror at first he uttered a curse, then he sat down and wept, tears flowed over his cheeks. He said to his companion: "To what end has my strength been renewed, to what end does my soul rejoice in its restoration? No benefit have I done to myself, to the earth lion is the benefit fallen." With dirges they wandered on till they came to the city of Erekh.

For the present cuneiform literature unfortunately tells us no more about this Island of the Blessed which so vividly calls to mind the Greek garden of the gods, Elysium, that Paradise in the western ocean where rose the springs of nectar and ambrosia. Neither do we hear of any other inhabitants of it, though it can hardly be supposed that the couple rescued from the Flood and their ferryman dwelt there entirely alone. It is, indeed, expressly stated that they lived "in the assembly of the gods." Thither fancy transferred other heroes of the people. Olympus was merged with Elysium by the Babylonians as later by the Greeks. Tiglath Pilesar expresses a hope that the great gods "have called the race of his priesthood to a dwelling-place on the mount of the gods for ever." According to the Gilgamesh epic he "who had fallen in battle with men" can claim a privileged lot after death. We are reminded of Walhalla when, at the close of the same epic, we read of the fate of the fallen as follows:

" On a pillow reposeth
 drinking pure water,
 he who was slain in battle;
 his father and his mother hold his head,
 and his wife [kneeleth] by his side (?)."

It is, perhaps, in a similar connection that we must interpret the close of a hymn, which runs:

" Glimmering water brought he in,"
 Ninzadim, the great jeweller of Anu,
 has to the care of his pure hands taken thee;
 Ea hath taken thee hence to the place of cleansing,
 to the place of cleansing hath he taken thee
 to (?) milk and honey he took thee,
 water of exorcism placed he in thy mouth,
 thy mouth he openeth by means of exorcism:
" Be clear as the heaven, be pure as the earth shine
   like the innermost part of heaven "

The Paradise of the First Created of Mankind in Eridu.

"At the mouth of the rivers," *i.e.*, where the Tigris and the Euphrates once flowed separately into the sea, Gilgamesh sought and found the entrance to the Island of the Blessed: "at the mouth of the rivers" also, holy water was procured for use in exorcism. Near this spot lay Eridu (the modern Abu-Shahrein, the Rata of the Ptolemies), the city of the cult of Ea, chief magician among the gods. The enchantment of Eridu plays a prominent part in the magical literature of the Babylonians. Now the mythology of the Gilgamesh epic points in many ways to the neighbourhood of Eridu and the activity of Ea, who, however, had temples also in Erekh and Surippak the actual scenes of the epic. "At the mouth of the rivers" must be sought likewise the garden of the gods where grew the enchanted tree bearing precious stones as fruit, and near to it the palace of the sea maiden who guarded the ferry over the Waters of Death. Close by dwelt the ferryman who took Gilgamesh across the water, led him to the fountain of healing and helped him to pluck the twigs from the tree of life. The ferryman, moreover, is called Arad-Ea, *i.e.*, "servant of Ea." It was Ea also who had rescued the hero's ancestor and his wife from the Flood. He must also have taken some part in the creation of the giant Eabani who had helped Gilgamesh in his exploits, for the name Eabani means "Ea creates." The miraculous healing to be found on the Island of the Blessed is another reference to the magic of the priests of Ea in Eridu.

These considerations have been advanced in detail because it will be seen that Eridu itself (or rather its cosmic archetype, all the great cities and temples of Babylonia having corresponding

CREATION OF ADAPA

cosmic originals (see page 24)) is represented as a kind of Paradise. At the conclusion of a spell in which the god of fire calls to his help Ea, the wise son of Eridu, we read:

" In Eridu grows a dusky palm in a pure place,
- its growth is superb, like lapis lazuli, it overshadows the ocean;
- the sojourn of Ea is in Eridu, overflowing with plenty,
- his dwelling is the place of the Underworld,
- his dwelling is the couch of the goddess Ba-u;
- within the splendid house, shady as the forest, none may enter."

An epical fragment lately discovered shows this Sanctuary of Eridu to have been the scene of the creation of Adapa by the god Ea. The account of the very act of creation has unfortunately not been preserved, but from similar descriptions in other specimens of cuneiform literature we are justified in assuming that Ea, the divine "potter," moulded his creature out of clay. Our fragment tells us that the god granted Adapa "divine authority, great discernment to order the laws of the land"; that he gave him wisdom—but did not give him everlasting life— and that he made him "the mighty one, the child of Eridu, to be the shepherd (?) of man." Further we learn that he was entrusted with various priestly functions and that he acted as baker and cup-bearer to the gods. With the baker of Eridu he superintended the baking, daily he provided Eridu with bread and water, with his own pure hand he attended to the platters, no platter was made ready without him, daily he embarked on his boat and went fishing for Eridu; when Ea stretched himself on his couch Adapa departed from Eridu and sailed about all night catching fish. From the fragments that relate the subsequent fate of Adapa we learn that Anu had been considering how the gift of eternal life could be given to this being who is in one passage distinctly called "Germ of mankind." With this episode we shall deal in the following section.

Food of Life and Water of Life in the Babylonian Paradise.

The epic fragments discovered at Tell el Amarna relate how Adapa was summoned before the throne of Anu, god of heaven, to answer for a deed of violence committed against the bird Zu, *i.e.*, the incarnation of the South wind. Anu's wrath being appeased he commanded a feast to be prepared for Adapa and festal raiment and oil for anointing to be given him. Garments and oil he accepted, but meat and drink he refused, for Ea had warned him: "When thou comest into the presence of Anu food of death will be offered thee, eat not thereof! Water of death will be offered thee, drink not thereof!" But lo! it was indeed food of life and water of life! Anu was filled with amazement. He had purposed that the man to whom his creator had revealed the inmost things of heaven and earth (*i.e.*, had bestowed on him the highest wisdom) should receive also the gift of immortality. By his refusal Adapa had defrauded himself of this gift. Therefore Anu commanded, "Take him and bring him back to his earth."

In this narrative food of life and water of life are supposed to be in the palace of the god of heaven. This also is a similar conception to that of Olympus and the Elysian Fields, for among the Greeks the source of the Olympian nectar and ambrosia was to be sought in the Paradise on the Western Ocean. Food of life and water of life were found also in the Babylonian Paradise "at the mouth of the rivers," in Eridu and on the Island of the Blessed. We have already told how Gilgamesh obtained healing by means of the water of the fountain of life and of the magic food on the Island of the Blessed, and how he found the magic plant of immortality. Obviously also, the divine baker and cup-bearer has not, in the mind of the narrator, to do with common food and drink, but with the Babylonian equivalents of nectar and ambrosia. The plant of life also, is occasionally mentioned elsewhere. "Delicate as the plant of life may his royal shepherdhood be," says the Assyrian king Rammanirari III., and Asarhaddon expresses the wish "that his royal rule may be favourable to the well-being of mankind, as is the plant of life." Frequent mention is made of the water of life, especially in the worship of Ea and Marduk, and the story of Adapa shows that this water was used for drinking and not merely for sprinkling and lustration. In the "Journey of Istar through Hades" express mention is made of drinking the water of life at the despatching of Uddushunamir, the messenger of the gods:

" Papsukal, the servant of the great gods, bowed his face before [Samas],
in mourning garb clothèd, with hair (?) dishevelled.
Samas stepped before Sin, his father, wee[ping],
before Ea the king his tears to pour forth:
Istar has gone down into the Underworld and has not returned thence."

After he has told how all generation on earth has been suspended because of this journey in Hades, it continues:

" Then Ea in the wisdom of his heart created a male being,
created Uddushunamir, the servant of the gods:

THE SACRED RIVERS

" Hail! Uddushunamir, turn thy face to the gate of the land without return,
the seven gates of the land without return, may they open before thee,
may Erishkigal see thee and welcome thee joyfully.
When her heart shall be calmed and her spirit cheered,
then conjure her in the name of the great gods.
Raise thou thy heads high, turn thy thoughts to the place of the spring (?), (and say):
" Hail! lady, may the spring (?) give me of its waters, thereof will I drink." ' "

Later, indeed, when the desire of the messenger has perforce been granted, the goddess of Hades says to her servant Namtar, " Sprinkle the goddess Istar with the water of life and send her away."

According to the exorcisms "holy water" was to be found " at the mouth of the rivers," *i.e.*, at the entrance to the Island of the Blessed on the shores of which was also the fountain of healing. The Euphrates and Tigris themselves were considered as sacred streams at the sources of which, as an historical inscription testifies, sacrifices were offered, and on the banks of which ceremonial ablutions were performed. Ea and his son Marduk were the lords of the water of life. At Ea's command the Underworld was forced to reveal its spring of the water of life, and elsewhere we read: " Go, my son Marduk, take the . . . one

FOOD AND WATER OF LIFE

... fetch water from the mouth of the two streams, into this water put thy pure spell, and consecrate it with thy pure spell, sprinkle [with the same water] man, the child of his god." Another passage runs: "Pure water [. . .], water of the Euphrates, that in the [. . .] place, water that is well hidden in the ocean, the pure mouth of Ea has purified it, the sons of the deep, the seven, they have made the water pure, clear and sparkling." According to a ritual text edited for the Assyrian royal worship the priest, clad in linen of Eridu, meets the king on the threshold of the "house of purification" and greets him in words that recall the blessing of Aaron!

"Ea make thee glad,
  Damkina, queen of the deep, illumine thee with her countenance,
  Marduk, the mighty overseer of the Igigi (heavenly spirits), exalt thy head."

Then the priest continued: "Their deeds endure on earth who take the holy message of Ea for their guide; the great gods of heaven come to his side, in the great sanctuaries of heaven and earth they come to his side; those chambers are pure and shining; in Ea's clear and shining water bathe the Anunaki, the great gods themselves purify their faces in it." Side by side with Ea, his son Marduk has command of the sacred water. In his temple was a holy fountain and frequent mention is made of Marduk's "vessel of purification," and of the "vessel of the decree of fate." This water may well have been represented at the great festival of the decree of fate, and it may be assumed that the vessel on wall sculptures and seal cylinders carried by winged genii to the tree of life represents the vessel of the water of life, and the fruit of the tree the corresponding food of life.

Conclusion.—Psychology of the Babylonian
Conceptions of Hades.

The Babylonian belief in a future life rested evidently in the first place on the conception of the soul as an individual entity, which forsakes the body at death. The body was regarded as done with (this belief is indicated, as we have seen, by the very word for corpse, *shalamtu, see* page 31), when with the last breath the soul had forsaken it. The soul therefore is called *napishtu* —*i.e.,* "breath," and it is said of a ghost which has been conjured up that he rises "like a breath of wind" out of the earth (page 30).

Among many peoples the conceptions of the world of the dead have been shaped according to the wishes and hopes raised in the minds of men as they muse on their own death, and look forward to life in an imaginary world full of pleasures denied them by the wretchedness of their life on earth. But among the Babylonians, as also among the Hebrews and the Greeks, representations of Hades reflect the melancholy thoughts roused in human souls by mourning for their dead. The soul of the dead sinks into a joyless existence, the misery of which has been foreshadowed by the phenomena of mortal sickness. The loss of a corporeal manifestation has already deprived it of all adornment and all exercise of the senses (page 9). Where is the soul to be found? Simplicity sought it in the tomb; the shade of the dead man finds it hard to part from the body which gave him form and substance. Hence the corpse was embalmed, and food and drink were placed in the grave. But imagination followed the fate of the soul beyond the tomb into a world of its own, the entrance to which lay in the West, whither also the sun journeyed before sinking down into darkness, and which was depicted as a faded counterpart of the world of men. That the more primitive conception of the dwelling of the soul in the grave still held its ground is to be explained by the demands of ancestor worship. In this cult the tombs were the places of offering, and its influence was stronger than any demands of logic.

DOCTRINE OF RETRIBUTION

Since to the Babylonians death and sojourn in Hades loomed as a dark fate indeed, there must soon have arisen in the soul of the people the thought that there might be distinctions in the fate of the dead, and retribution in the next world. It must also have appeared impossible that the ethical system of things taken for granted in Babylonian hymns and prayers should be entirely done away with beyond the tomb. Some traces of a doctrine of retribution are, as a matter of fact, to be found in the Babylonian representations of Hades. What is the goddess scribe of the Underworld writing as she stands bending before the goddess of Hades (p. 23)? What is the significance of the arrangements by which the strength of an unwelcome intruder was to be broken (p. 21)? Why were the Anunaki set upon a golden throne when decision was to be made as to whether Istar should go free? Does it not seem as though they exercised judicial functions after the manner of the forty-two judges at the Judgment of Osiris? In an exorcism on one of the Hades reliefs, mention is made of the "Judgment of the life of the great gods." The fact that individual favourites of the gods were removed to a happy life on some Island of the Blessed or elsewhere in the vicinity of the gods is no proof of a belief in the separation of good and evil after death, but it does testify that the Babylonians in their meditations on death and the grave refused to give up all ἡδυστέρας ἐλπίδας, "sweeter hopes," and that they attributed to their gods a power over the fate of man's soul extending beyond the tomb.

BIBLIOGRAPHICAL APPENDIX.

Alfred Jeremias, "Die Babylonisch-assyrischen Vorstellungen vom Leben nach dem Tode (mit Berücksichtigung der alttestamentlichen Parallelen)." Leipzig. J. C. Hinrichs (1887). 6s.

P. Jensen, "Kosmologie der Babylonier." Strassburg (1890). 40s.

Alfred Jeremias, article "Nergal" in *Roscher's Lexicon der Mythologie*, vol. iii. col. 250 *et seq.*

Bruno Meissner, "Babylonisch Leichenfeierlichkeiten (*Wiener Zeitschr. f. d. Kunde des Morgenlandes* vol. xii. p. 59 *et seq.*

Scheil, "Relief représentant une scène funéraire babylonienne" (*Recueil de Travaux relatif à la Philologie et à l'Archéologie égyptiennes et assyriennes*, vol. xx. p. 5.

Messerschmidt, "Ein vergessenes Hades-Relief" (*Orientalistische Lit. Zeitung*, 1901, p. 175).

F. Thureau-Dangin, "Inscription provenant d'un tombeau babylonien" (*Orientalistische Lit. Zeitung*, 1901, p. 5).

Schwally, "Das Leben nach dem Tode nach den Vorstellungen des alten Israels." Giessen (1892). (A useful summary of purely Jewish ideas, but written without knowledge of, or reference to, the Babylonian evidence.) 5s.

BIBLIOGRAPHICAL APPENDIX

Frey, Johs. Tod, "Seelenglaube und Seelenkult im alten Israel." Leipzig (1898). (Makes no use of Babylonian evidence.) 4s.

The translations of the Gilgamesh (Nimrod) epos by Alfred Jeremias: "Izdubar-Nimrud," Leipzig, 1891 (*cf.* also his articles "Ishtar," "Izdubar," in Roscher's "Lexicon"), and P. Jensen, *Keilnischriftliche Bibliothek*, Bd. vi. "Die alt-babylonische Epen und Mythen" may also be consulted. See also the articles "Creation," "Deluge," "Eschatology," "Nimrod," and "Paradise," in the "Encyclopædia Biblica," edited by the Rev. Dr. Cheyne and J. S. Black, and in Rev. Dr. J. Hastings' "Dictionary of the Bible."

www.ingramcontent.com/pod-product-compliance
Lightning Source LLC
Chambersburg PA
CBHW061514040426
42450CB00008B/1611